Thank you for investing

My
Gratitude Attitu.
Journal

A positive investment in your future towards creating the life you want.
Practising gratitude is the greatest gift you can give to yourself. Spending just 5
minutes a day writing in 'My Gratitude Attitude Journal' can increase your long-
term well-being by more than 10 percent. That's the same impact as doubling your
income! It's been scientifically proven to help us bounce back from stress quicker;
improve our self esteem, career, health and relationships. Even allowing us to get
asleep faster.

My own story of overcoming multiple sclerosis and living symptom free without
medication is hugely attributed to practising gratitude. A daily routine of writing as
soon as I wake has had a profoundly positive effect on my life. This drives my passion
to share this beautiful and simple practice with you.

Sign up to my mailing list for gratitude journaling exercises & ideas. Let's get going!

Karen
Dwyer
xx

Find us on
f ⛄ 📷 🐦

www.mygratitudeattitudejournal.com
karen@mygratitudeattitudejournal.com

This gratitude attitude journal belongs to:

_____

WHAT DO YOU WANT TO ACHIEVE FROM PRACTICING GRATITUDE EVERYDAY?

_____

_____

HERE'S AN EXAMPLE OF MY DAILY GRATITUDE

WHAT ARE YOU GRATEFUL FOR

Monday

1. My 2 incredible daughters and family

2. My healthy body, free of MS

3. My sister for designing this journal ;)

TOP TASK TODAY Walk 10,000 steps ✔

Week 2

WHAT ARE YOU GRATEFUL FOR

Monday

1. _____

2. _____

3. _____

TOP TASK TODAY _____ ☐

WHAT ARE YOU GRATEFUL FOR

Tuesday

1. _____

2. _____

3. _____

TOP TASK TODAY _____ ☐

WHAT ARE YOU GRATEFUL FOR

Wednesday

1. _____

2. _____

3. _____

TOP TASK TODAY _____ ☐

WHAT ARE YOU GRATEFUL FOR

Thursday

1. _____

2. _____

3. _____

TOP TASK TODAY _____ ☐

"Don't expect to see a change if you don't make one."
John Assaraf

Friday

WHAT ARE YOU GRATEFUL FOR

1. _____

2. _____

3. _____

TOP TASK TODAY _____ ☐

Saturday

WHAT ARE YOU GRATEFUL FOR

1. _____

2. _____

3. _____

TOP TASK TODAY _____ ☐

Sunday

WHAT ARE YOU GRATEFUL FOR

1. _____

2. _____

3. _____

TOP TASK TODAY _____ ☐

Notes

Week 3

WHAT ARE YOU GRATEFUL FOR

Monday

1. _____

2. _____

3. _____

TOP TASK TODAY _____ ☐

WHAT ARE YOU GRATEFUL FOR

Tuesday

1. _____

2. _____

3. _____

TOP TASK TODAY _____ ☐

WHAT ARE YOU GRATEFUL FOR

Wednesday

1. _____

2. _____

3. _____

TOP TASK TODAY _____ ☐

WHAT ARE YOU GRATEFUL FOR

Thursday

1. _____

2. _____

3. _____

TOP TASK TODAY _____ ☐

"Impossible things can happen as a result of your dreams."
COL CHRIS HADFIELD

/ / 20

Friday

WHAT ARE YOU GRATEFUL FOR

1. _____
2. _____
3. _____

TOP TASK TODAY _____ ☐

Saturday

WHAT ARE YOU GRATEFUL FOR

1. _____
2. _____
3. _____

TOP TASK TODAY _____ ☐

Sunday

WHAT ARE YOU GRATEFUL FOR

1. _____
2. _____
3. _____

TOP TASK TODAY _____ ☐

Notes

Week 4

WHAT ARE YOU GRATEFUL FOR

Monday

1. _____

2. _____

3. _____

TOP TASK TODAY _____ ☐

WHAT ARE YOU GRATEFUL FOR

Tuesday

1. _____

2. _____

3. _____

TOP TASK TODAY _____ ☐

WHAT ARE YOU GRATEFUL FOR

Wednesday

1. _____

2. _____

3. _____

TOP TASK TODAY _____ ☐

WHAT ARE YOU GRATEFUL FOR

Thursday

1. _____

2. _____

3. _____

TOP TASK TODAY _____ ☐

"A great attitude becomes a great day which becomes a great month which becomes
a great year which becomes a great life." Mandy Hale

WHAT ARE YOU GRATEFUL FOR

Friday

1. _____

2. _____

3. _____

TOP TASK TODAY _____ ☐

WHAT ARE YOU GRATEFUL FOR

Saturday

1. _____

2. _____

3. _____

TOP TASK TODAY _____ ☐

WHAT ARE YOU GRATEFUL FOR

Sunday

1. _____

2. _____

3. _____

TOP TASK TODAY _____ ☐

Notes

Week 5

WHAT ARE YOU GRATEFUL FOR   *Monday*

1. _____

2. _____

3. _____

TOP TASK TODAY _____ ☐

WHAT ARE YOU GRATEFUL FOR   *Tuesday*

1. _____

2. _____

3. _____

TOP TASK TODAY _____ ☐

WHAT ARE YOU GRATEFUL FOR   *Wednesday*

1. _____

2. _____

3. _____

TOP TASK TODAY _____ ☐

WHAT ARE YOU GRATEFUL FOR   *Thursday*

1. _____

2. _____

3. _____

TOP TASK TODAY _____ ☐

"Life is like a camera, focus on what's important, capture the good times, develop from the negatives and if things don't work out, take another shot"

Friday

WHAT ARE YOU GRATEFUL FOR

1. _____

2. _____

3. _____

TOP TASK TODAY _____ ☐

Saturday

WHAT ARE YOU GRATEFUL FOR

1. _____

2. _____

3. _____

TOP TASK TODAY _____ ☐

Sunday

WHAT ARE YOU GRATEFUL FOR

1. _____

2. _____

3. _____

TOP TASK TODAY _____ ☐

Notes

Week 6

WHAT ARE YOU GRATEFUL FOR

Monday

1. _____

2. _____

3. _____

TOP TASK TODAY _____ ☐

WHAT ARE YOU GRATEFUL FOR

Tuesday

1. _____

2. _____

3. _____

TOP TASK TODAY _____ ☐

WHAT ARE YOU GRATEFUL FOR

Wednesday

1. _____

2. _____

3. _____

TOP TASK TODAY _____ ☐

WHAT ARE YOU GRATEFUL FOR

Thursday

1. _____

2. _____

3. _____

TOP TASK TODAY _____ ☐

"There's a positive lesson in every negative."
Karen Dwyer

WHAT ARE YOU GRATEFUL FOR

Friday

1. _____

2. _____

3. _____

TOP TASK TODAY _____ ☐

WHAT ARE YOU GRATEFUL FOR

Saturday

1. _____

2. _____

3. _____

TOP TASK TODAY _____ ☐

WHAT ARE YOU GRATEFUL FOR

Sunday

1. _____

2. _____

3. _____

TOP TASK TODAY _____ ☐

Notes

Week 7

WHAT ARE YOU GRATEFUL FOR

Monday

1. _____

2. _____

3. _____

TOP TASK TODAY _____ ☐

WHAT ARE YOU GRATEFUL FOR

Tuesday

1. _____

2. _____

3. _____

TOP TASK TODAY _____ ☐

WHAT ARE YOU GRATEFUL FOR

Wednesday

1. _____

2. _____

3. _____

TOP TASK TODAY _____ ☐

WHAT ARE YOU GRATEFUL FOR

Thursday

1. _____

2. _____

3. _____

TOP TASK TODAY _____ ☐

"Talk to yourself like you would to someone you love."
Brené Brown

WHAT ARE YOU GRATEFUL FOR

Friday

1. _____

2. _____

3. _____

TOP TASK TODAY _____ ☐

WHAT ARE YOU GRATEFUL FOR

Saturday

1. _____

2. _____

3. _____

TOP TASK TODAY _____ ☐

WHAT ARE YOU GRATEFUL FOR

Sunday

1. _____

2. _____

3. _____

TOP TASK TODAY _____ ☐

Notes

Week 8

WHAT ARE YOU GRATEFUL FOR   *Monday*

1. _____

2. _____

3. _____

TOP TASK TODAY _____ ☐

WHAT ARE YOU GRATEFUL FOR   *Tuesday*

1. _____

2. _____

3. _____

TOP TASK TODAY _____ ☐

WHAT ARE YOU GRATEFUL FOR   *Wednesday*

1. _____

2. _____

3. _____

TOP TASK TODAY _____ ☐

WHAT ARE YOU GRATEFUL FOR   *Thursday*

1. _____

2. _____

3. _____

TOP TASK TODAY _____ ☐

"Decide what you want. Believe you can have it. Believe you deserve it an believe it's possible for you." Jack Canfield

/ / 20

Friday

WHAT ARE YOU GRATEFUL FOR

1. _____

2. _____

3. _____

TOP TASK TODAY _____ ☐

WHAT ARE YOU GRATEFUL FOR

Saturday

1. _____

2. _____

3. _____

TOP TASK TODAY _____ ☐

WHAT ARE YOU GRATEFUL FOR

Sunday

1. _____

2. _____

3. _____

TOP TASK TODAY _____ ☐

Notes

Week 9

WHAT ARE YOU GRATEFUL FOR

Monday

1. _____

2. _____

3. _____

TOP TASK TODAY _____ ☐

WHAT ARE YOU GRATEFUL FOR

Tuesday

1. _____

2. _____

3. _____

TOP TASK TODAY _____ ☐

WHAT ARE YOU GRATEFUL FOR

Wednesday

1. _____

2. _____

3. _____

TOP TASK TODAY _____ ☐

WHAT ARE YOU GRATEFUL FOR

Thursday

1. _____

2. _____

3. _____

TOP TASK TODAY _____ ☐

"You gain strength, courage and confidence in every experience in which you really stop to look fear in the face." Eleanor Roosevelt

Friday

WHAT ARE YOU GRATEFUL FOR

1. _____

2. _____

3. _____

TOP TASK TODAY _____ ☐

Saturday

WHAT ARE YOU GRATEFUL FOR

1. _____

2. _____

3. _____

TOP TASK TODAY _____ ☐

Sunday

WHAT ARE YOU GRATEFUL FOR

1. _____

2. _____

3. _____

TOP TASK TODAY _____ ☐

Notes

Week 10

WHAT ARE YOU GRATEFUL FOR

Monday

1. _____

2. _____

3. _____

TOP TASK TODAY _____ ☐

WHAT ARE YOU GRATEFUL FOR

Tuesday

1. _____

2. _____

3. _____

TOP TASK TODAY _____ ☐

WHAT ARE YOU GRATEFUL FOR

Wednesday

1. _____

2. _____

3. _____

TOP TASK TODAY _____ ☐

WHAT ARE YOU GRATEFUL FOR

Thursday

1. _____

2. _____

3. _____

TOP TASK TODAY _____ ☐

"Decide what you want. Believe you can have it. Believe you deserve it an believe it's possible for you." Jack Canfield

WHAT ARE YOU GRATEFUL FOR

Friday

1. _____

2. _____

3. _____

TOP TASK TODAY _____ ☐

WHAT ARE YOU GRATEFUL FOR

Saturday

1. _____

2. _____

3. _____

TOP TASK TODAY _____ ☐

WHAT ARE YOU GRATEFUL FOR

Sunday

1. _____

2. _____

3. _____

TOP TASK TODAY _____ ☐

Notes

Week 11

WHAT ARE YOU GRATEFUL FOR $\qquad$ *Monday*

1. _____

2. _____

3. _____

TOP TASK TODAY _____ ☐

WHAT ARE YOU GRATEFUL FOR $\qquad$ *Tuesday*

1. _____

2. _____

3. _____

TOP TASK TODAY _____ ☐

WHAT ARE YOU GRATEFUL FOR $\qquad$ *Wednesday*

1. _____

2. _____

3. _____

TOP TASK TODAY _____ ☐

WHAT ARE YOU GRATEFUL FOR $\qquad$ *Thursday*

1. _____

2. _____

3. _____

TOP TASK TODAY _____ ☐

"Let us be grateful to the people who make us happy; they are the charming gardeners who make our souls blossom." Marcel Proust

Friday

WHAT ARE YOU GRATEFUL FOR

1. _____

2. _____

3. _____

TOP TASK TODAY _____ ☐

Saturday

WHAT ARE YOU GRATEFUL FOR

1. _____

2. _____

3. _____

TOP TASK TODAY _____ ☐

Sunday

WHAT ARE YOU GRATEFUL FOR

1. _____

2. _____

3. _____

TOP TASK TODAY _____ ☐

Notes

Week 12

WHAT ARE YOU GRATEFUL FOR

Monday

1. _____

2. _____

3. _____

TOP TASK TODAY _____ ☐

WHAT ARE YOU GRATEFUL FOR

Tuesday

1. _____

2. _____

3. _____

TOP TASK TODAY _____ ☐

WHAT ARE YOU GRATEFUL FOR

Wednesday

1. _____

2. _____

3. _____

TOP TASK TODAY _____ ☐

WHAT ARE YOU GRATEFUL FOR

Thursday

1. _____

2. _____

3. _____

TOP TASK TODAY _____ ☐

Do not spoil what you have by desiring what you have not; remember that what you now have was once among the things you only hoped for." Epicurus

WHAT ARE YOU GRATEFUL FOR

Friday

1. _____

2. _____

3. _____

TOP TASK TODAY _____ ☐

WHAT ARE YOU GRATEFUL FOR

Saturday

1. _____

2. _____

3. _____

TOP TASK TODAY _____ ☐

WHAT ARE YOU GRATEFUL FOR

Sunday

1. _____

2. _____

3. _____

TOP TASK TODAY _____ ☐

Notes

Week 13

WHAT ARE YOU GRATEFUL FOR

Monday

1. _____

2. _____

3. _____

TOP TASK TODAY _____ ☐

WHAT ARE YOU GRATEFUL FOR

Tuesday

1. _____

2. _____

3. _____

TOP TASK TODAY _____ ☐

WHAT ARE YOU GRATEFUL FOR

Wednesday

1. _____

2. _____

3. _____

TOP TASK TODAY _____ ☐

WHAT ARE YOU GRATEFUL FOR

Thursday

1. _____

2. _____

3. _____

TOP TASK TODAY _____ ☐

"Sometimes life knocks you on your ass... get up, get up, get up!!! Happiness is not the absence of problems, it's the ability to deal with them." Steve Maraboli

WHAT ARE YOU GRATEFUL FOR

Friday

1. _____

2. _____

3. _____

TOP TASK TODAY _____ ☐

WHAT ARE YOU GRATEFUL FOR

Saturday

1. _____

2. _____

3. _____

TOP TASK TODAY _____ ☐

WHAT ARE YOU GRATEFUL FOR

Sunday

1. _____

2. _____

3. _____

TOP TASK TODAY _____ ☐

Notes

Reflections

WHAT HAS YOUR GRATITUDE PRACTICE BROUGHT YOU?

WHAT ARE YOU GOING TO CHANGE?

WHAT'S YOUR NUMBER ONE LESSON?

WHAT WOULD YOU LIKE TO ACHIEVE NEXT?

Find us on

Week 14

WHAT ARE YOU GRATEFUL FOR
Monday

1. _____

2. _____

3. _____

TOP TASK TODAY _____ ☐

WHAT ARE YOU GRATEFUL FOR
Tuesday

1. _____

2. _____

3. _____

TOP TASK TODAY _____ ☐

WHAT ARE YOU GRATEFUL FOR
Wednesday

1. _____

2. _____

3. _____

TOP TASK TODAY _____ ☐

WHAT ARE YOU GRATEFUL FOR
Thursday

1. _____

2. _____

3. _____

TOP TASK TODAY _____ ☐

"Respond to every call that ignites your spirit."
Rumi

WHAT ARE YOU GRATEFUL FOR

Friday

1. _____

2. _____

3. _____

TOP TASK TODAY _____ ☐

WHAT ARE YOU GRATEFUL FOR

Saturday

1. _____

2. _____

3. _____

TOP TASK TODAY _____ ☐

WHAT ARE YOU GRATEFUL FOR

Sunday

1. _____

2. _____

3. _____

TOP TASK TODAY _____ ☐

Notes

Week 15

WHAT ARE YOU GRATEFUL FOR

Monday

1. _____

2. _____

3. _____

TOP TASK TODAY _____ ☐

WHAT ARE YOU GRATEFUL FOR

Tuesday

1. _____

2. _____

3. _____

TOP TASK TODAY _____ ☐

WHAT ARE YOU GRATEFUL FOR

Wednesday

1. _____

2. _____

3. _____

TOP TASK TODAY _____ ☐

WHAT ARE YOU GRATEFUL FOR

Thursday

1. _____

2. _____

3. _____

TOP TASK TODAY _____ ☐

"Piglet noticed that even though he had a Very Small Heart, it could hold a rather large amount of Gratitude." A.A. Milne Emerson

WHAT ARE YOU GRATEFUL FOR

Friday

1. _____

2. _____

3. _____

TOP TASK TODAY _____ ☐

WHAT ARE YOU GRATEFUL FOR

Saturday

1. _____

2. _____

3. _____

TOP TASK TODAY _____ ☐

WHAT ARE YOU GRATEFUL FOR

Sunday

1. _____

2. _____

3. _____

TOP TASK TODAY _____ ☐

Notes

Week 16

WHAT ARE YOU GRATEFUL FOR

Monday

1. _____

2. _____

3. _____

TOP TASK TODAY _____ ☐

WHAT ARE YOU GRATEFUL FOR

Tuesday

1. _____

2. _____

3. _____

TOP TASK TODAY _____ ☐

WHAT ARE YOU GRATEFUL FOR

Wednesday

1. _____

2. _____

3. _____

TOP TASK TODAY _____ ☐

WHAT ARE YOU GRATEFUL FOR

Thursday

1. _____

2. _____

3. _____

TOP TASK TODAY _____ ☐

"Let gratitude be the pillow upon which you kneel to say your nightly prayer.
And let faith be the bridge you build to overcome evil and welcome good." Maya Angelou

WHAT ARE YOU GRATEFUL FOR

Friday

1. _____

2. _____

3. _____

TOP TASK TODAY _____ ☐

WHAT ARE YOU GRATEFUL FOR

Saturday

1. _____

2. _____

3. _____

TOP TASK TODAY _____ ☐

WHAT ARE YOU GRATEFUL FOR

Sunday

1. _____

2. _____

3. _____

TOP TASK TODAY _____ ☐

Notes

Week 17

WHAT ARE YOU GRATEFUL FOR

Monday

1. _____

2. _____

3. _____

TOP TASK TODAY _____ ☐

WHAT ARE YOU GRATEFUL FOR

Tuesday

1. _____

2. _____

3. _____

TOP TASK TODAY _____ ☐

WHAT ARE YOU GRATEFUL FOR

Wednesday

1. _____

2. _____

3. _____

TOP TASK TODAY _____ ☐

WHAT ARE YOU GRATEFUL FOR

Thursday

1. _____

2. _____

3. _____

TOP TASK TODAY _____ ☐

"If the only prayer you said was thank you, that would be enough." Meister Eckhart

WHAT ARE YOU GRATEFUL FOR

Friday

1. _____

2. _____

3. _____

TOP TASK TODAY _____ ☐

WHAT ARE YOU GRATEFUL FOR

Saturday

1. _____

2. _____

3. _____

TOP TASK TODAY _____ ☐

WHAT ARE YOU GRATEFUL FOR

Sunday

1. _____

2. _____

3. _____

TOP TASK TODAY _____ ☐

Notes

Week 18

WHAT ARE YOU GRATEFUL FOR

Monday

1. _____

2. _____

3. _____

TOP TASK TODAY _____ ☐

WHAT ARE YOU GRATEFUL FOR

Tuesday

1. _____

2. _____

3. _____

TOP TASK TODAY _____ ☐

WHAT ARE YOU GRATEFUL FOR

Wednesday

1. _____

2. _____

3. _____

TOP TASK TODAY _____ ☐

WHAT ARE YOU GRATEFUL FOR

Thursday

1. _____

2. _____

3. _____

TOP TASK TODAY _____ ☐

"Some people grumble that roses have thorns; I am grateful that thorns have roses."
Alphonse Karr

WHAT ARE YOU GRATEFUL FOR

Friday

1. _____

2. _____

3. _____

TOP TASK TODAY _____ ☐

WHAT ARE YOU GRATEFUL FOR

Saturday

1. _____

2. _____

3. _____

TOP TASK TODAY _____ ☐

WHAT ARE YOU GRATEFUL FOR

Sunday

1. _____

2. _____

3. _____

TOP TASK TODAY _____ ☐

Notes

Week 19

WHAT ARE YOU GRATEFUL FOR

Monday

1. _____

2. _____

3. _____

TOP TASK TODAY _____ ☐

WHAT ARE YOU GRATEFUL FOR

Tuesday

1. _____

2. _____

3. _____

TOP TASK TODAY _____ ☐

WHAT ARE YOU GRATEFUL FOR

Wednesday

1. _____

2. _____

3. _____

TOP TASK TODAY _____ ☐

WHAT ARE YOU GRATEFUL FOR

Thursday

1. _____

2. _____

3. _____

TOP TASK TODAY _____ ☐

"Great things happen to those who don't stop believing, trying, learning, and being grateful." Roy T. Bennett

Friday

WHAT ARE YOU GRATEFUL FOR

1. _____

2. _____

3. _____

TOP TASK TODAY _____ ☐

Saturday

WHAT ARE YOU GRATEFUL FOR

1. _____

2. _____

3. _____

TOP TASK TODAY _____ ☐

Sunday

WHAT ARE YOU GRATEFUL FOR

1. _____

2. _____

3. _____

TOP TASK TODAY _____ ☐

Notes

Week 20

WHAT ARE YOU GRATEFUL FOR

Monday

1. _____

2. _____

3. _____

TOP TASK TODAY _____ ☐

WHAT ARE YOU GRATEFUL FOR

Tuesday

1. _____

2. _____

3. _____

TOP TASK TODAY _____ ☐

WHAT ARE YOU GRATEFUL FOR

Wednesday

1. _____

2. _____

3. _____

TOP TASK TODAY _____ ☐

WHAT ARE YOU GRATEFUL FOR

Thursday

1. _____

2. _____

3. _____

TOP TASK TODAY _____ ☐

"Gratitude is not only the greatest of virtues, but the parent of all others."
Marcus Tullius Cicero

WHAT ARE YOU GRATEFUL FOR

Friday

1. _____

2. _____

3. _____

TOP TASK TODAY _____ ☐

WHAT ARE YOU GRATEFUL FOR

Saturday

1. _____

2. _____

3. _____

TOP TASK TODAY _____ ☐

WHAT ARE YOU GRATEFUL FOR

Sunday

1. _____

2. _____

3. _____

TOP TASK TODAY _____ ☐

Notes

Week 21

WHAT ARE YOU GRATEFUL FOR   Monday

1. _____

2. _____

3. _____

TOP TASK TODAY _____ ☐

WHAT ARE YOU GRATEFUL FOR   Tuesday

1. _____

2. _____

3. _____

TOP TASK TODAY _____ ☐

WHAT ARE YOU GRATEFUL FOR   Wednesday

1. _____

2. _____

3. _____

TOP TASK TODAY _____ ☐

WHAT ARE YOU GRATEFUL FOR   Thursday

1. _____

2. _____

3. _____

TOP TASK TODAY _____ ☐

"When you arise in the morning, think of what a precious privilege it is to be alive-to breathe, to think, to enjoy, to love—then make that day count!" Steve Maraboli

WHAT ARE YOU GRATEFUL FOR

Friday

1. _____

2. _____

3. _____

TOP TASK TODAY _____ ☐

WHAT ARE YOU GRATEFUL FOR

Saturday

1. _____

2. _____

3. _____

TOP TASK TODAY _____ ☐

WHAT ARE YOU GRATEFUL FOR

Sunday

1. _____

2. _____

3. _____

TOP TASK TODAY _____ ☐

Notes

Week 22

WHAT ARE YOU GRATEFUL FOR

Monday

1. _____

2. _____

3. _____

TOP TASK TODAY _____ ☐

WHAT ARE YOU GRATEFUL FOR

Tuesday

1. _____

2. _____

3. _____

TOP TASK TODAY _____ ☐

WHAT ARE YOU GRATEFUL FOR

Wednesday

1. _____

2. _____

3. _____

TOP TASK TODAY _____ ☐

WHAT ARE YOU GRATEFUL FOR

Thursday

1. _____

2. _____

3. _____

TOP TASK TODAY _____ ☐

"The highest tribute to the dead is not grief but gratitude."
Thornton Wilder

WHAT ARE YOU GRATEFUL FOR

Friday

1. _____

2. _____

3. _____

TOP TASK TODAY _____ ☐

WHAT ARE YOU GRATEFUL FOR

Saturday

1. _____

2. _____

3. _____

TOP TASK TODAY _____ ☐

WHAT ARE YOU GRATEFUL FOR

Sunday

1. _____

2. _____

3. _____

TOP TASK TODAY _____ ☐

Notes

Week 23

WHAT ARE YOU GRATEFUL FOR

Monday

1. _____

2. _____

3. _____

TOP TASK TODAY _____ ☐

WHAT ARE YOU GRATEFUL FOR

Tuesday

1. _____

2. _____

3. _____

TOP TASK TODAY _____ ☐

WHAT ARE YOU GRATEFUL FOR

Wednesday

1. _____

2. _____

3. _____

TOP TASK TODAY _____ ☐

WHAT ARE YOU GRATEFUL FOR

Thursday

1. _____

2. _____

3. _____

TOP TASK TODAY _____ ☐

"Gratitude can transform common days into thanksgivings, turn routine jobs into joy, and change ordinary opportunities into blessings." William Arthur Ward

WHAT ARE YOU GRATEFUL FOR

Friday

1. _____

2. _____

3. _____

TOP TASK TODAY _____ ☐

WHAT ARE YOU GRATEFUL FOR

Saturday

1. _____

2. _____

3. _____

TOP TASK TODAY _____ ☐

WHAT ARE YOU GRATEFUL FOR

Sunday

1. _____

2. _____

3. _____

TOP TASK TODAY _____ ☐

Notes

Week 24

WHAT ARE YOU GRATEFUL FOR

Monday

1. _____

2. _____

3. _____

TOP TASK TODAY _____ ☐

WHAT ARE YOU GRATEFUL FOR

Tuesday

1. _____

2. _____

3. _____

TOP TASK TODAY _____ ☐

WHAT ARE YOU GRATEFUL FOR

Wednesday

1. _____

2. _____

3. _____

TOP TASK TODAY _____ ☐

WHAT ARE YOU GRATEFUL FOR

Thursday

1. _____

2. _____

3. _____

TOP TASK TODAY _____ ☐

"Feeling gratitude and not expressing it is like wrapping a present and not giving it."
William Arthur Ward

WHAT ARE YOU GRATEFUL FOR

Friday

1. _____

2. _____

3. _____

TOP TASK TODAY _____ ☐

WHAT ARE YOU GRATEFUL FOR

Saturday

1. _____

2. _____

3. _____

TOP TASK TODAY _____ ☐

WHAT ARE YOU GRATEFUL FOR

Sunday

1. _____

2. _____

3. _____

TOP TASK TODAY _____ ☐

Notes

Week 25

WHAT ARE YOU GRATEFUL FOR
Monday

1. _____

2. _____

3. _____

TOP TASK TODAY _____ ☐

WHAT ARE YOU GRATEFUL FOR
Tuesday

1. _____

2. _____

3. _____

TOP TASK TODAY _____ ☐

WHAT ARE YOU GRATEFUL FOR
Wednesday

1. _____

2. _____

3. _____

TOP TASK TODAY _____ ☐

WHAT ARE YOU GRATEFUL FOR
Thursday

1. _____

2. _____

3. _____

TOP TASK TODAY _____ ☐

"In ordinary life we hardly realize that we receive a great deal more than we give, and that it is only with gratitude that life becomes rich." Dietrich Bonhoeffer

WHAT ARE YOU GRATEFUL FOR

Friday

1. _____

2. _____

3. _____

TOP TASK TODAY _____ ☐

WHAT ARE YOU GRATEFUL FOR

Saturday

1. _____

2. _____

3. _____

TOP TASK TODAY _____ ☐

WHAT ARE YOU GRATEFUL FOR

Sunday

1. _____

2. _____

3. _____

TOP TASK TODAY _____ ☐

Notes

Week 26

WHAT ARE YOU GRATEFUL FOR

Monday

1. _____

2. _____

3. _____

TOP TASK TODAY _____ ☐

WHAT ARE YOU GRATEFUL FOR

Tuesday

1. _____

2. _____

3. _____

TOP TASK TODAY _____ ☐

WHAT ARE YOU GRATEFUL FOR

Wednesday

1. _____

2. _____

3. _____

TOP TASK TODAY _____ ☐

WHAT ARE YOU GRATEFUL FOR

Thursday

1. _____

2. _____

3. _____

TOP TASK TODAY _____ ☐

"Whatever you appreciate and give thanks for will increase in your life." Sanaya Roman

Friday

WHAT ARE YOU GRATEFUL FOR

1. _____

2. _____

3. _____

TOP TASK TODAY _____ ☐

Saturday

WHAT ARE YOU GRATEFUL FOR

1. _____

2. _____

3. _____

TOP TASK TODAY _____ ☐

Sunday

WHAT ARE YOU GRATEFUL FOR

1. _____

2. _____

3. _____

TOP TASK TODAY _____ ☐

Notes

Reflections

WHAT HAS YOUR GRATITUDE PRACTICE BROUGHT YOU?

WHAT ARE YOU GOING TO CHANGE?

WHAT'S YOUR NUMBER ONE LESSON?

WHAT WOULD YOU LIKE TO ACHIEVE NEXT?

Find us on **f** 👻 📷 🐦

Week 27

WHAT ARE YOU GRATEFUL FOR

Monday

1. _____

2. _____

3. _____

TOP TASK TODAY _____ ☐

WHAT ARE YOU GRATEFUL FOR

Tuesday

1. _____

2. _____

3. _____

TOP TASK TODAY _____ ☐

WHAT ARE YOU GRATEFUL FOR

Wednesday

1. _____

2. _____

3. _____

TOP TASK TODAY _____ ☐

WHAT ARE YOU GRATEFUL FOR

Thursday

1. _____

2. _____

3. _____

TOP TASK TODAY _____ ☐

"When it comes to life the critical thing is whether you take things for granted or take them with gratitude." G.K. Chesterton

WHAT ARE YOU GRATEFUL FOR

Friday

1. _____

2. _____

3. _____

TOP TASK TODAY _____ ☐

WHAT ARE YOU GRATEFUL FOR

Saturday

1. _____

2. _____

3. _____

TOP TASK TODAY _____ ☐

WHAT ARE YOU GRATEFUL FOR

Sunday

1. _____

2. _____

3. _____

TOP TASK TODAY _____ ☐

Notes

Week 28

WHAT ARE YOU GRATEFUL FOR

Monday

1. _____

2. _____

3. _____

TOP TASK TODAY _____ ☐

WHAT ARE YOU GRATEFUL FOR

Tuesday

1. _____

2. _____

3. _____

TOP TASK TODAY _____ ☐

WHAT ARE YOU GRATEFUL FOR

Wednesday

1. _____

2. _____

3. _____

TOP TASK TODAY _____ ☐

WHAT ARE YOU GRATEFUL FOR

Thursday

1. _____

2. _____

3. _____

TOP TASK TODAY _____ ☐

"Gratitude for the seemingly insignificant—a seed—this plants the giant miracle."
Ann Voskamp

WHAT ARE YOU GRATEFUL FOR

Friday

1. _____

2. _____

3. _____

TOP TASK TODAY _____ ☐

WHAT ARE YOU GRATEFUL FOR

Saturday

1. _____

2. _____

3. _____

TOP TASK TODAY _____ ☐

WHAT ARE YOU GRATEFUL FOR

Sunday

1. _____

2. _____

3. _____

TOP TASK TODAY _____ ☐

Notes

Week 29

WHAT ARE YOU GRATEFUL FOR

Monday

1. _____

2. _____

3. _____

TOP TASK TODAY _____ ☐

WHAT ARE YOU GRATEFUL FOR

Tuesday

1. _____

2. _____

3. _____

TOP TASK TODAY _____ ☐

WHAT ARE YOU GRATEFUL FOR

Wednesday

1. _____

2. _____

3. _____

TOP TASK TODAY _____ ☐

WHAT ARE YOU GRATEFUL FOR

Thursday

1. _____

2. _____

3. _____

TOP TASK TODAY _____ ☐

"The soul that gives thanks can find comfort in everything; the soul that complains can find comfort in nothing." Hannah Whitall Smith

WHAT ARE YOU GRATEFUL FOR

Friday

1. _____

2. _____

3. _____

TOP TASK TODAY _____ ☐

WHAT ARE YOU GRATEFUL FOR

Saturday

1. _____

2. _____

3. _____

TOP TASK TODAY _____ ☐

WHAT ARE YOU GRATEFUL FOR

Sunday

1. _____

2. _____

3. _____

TOP TASK TODAY _____ ☐

Notes

Week 30

WHAT ARE YOU GRATEFUL FOR

Monday

1. _____

2. _____

3. _____

TOP TASK TODAY _____ ☐

WHAT ARE YOU GRATEFUL FOR

Tuesday

1. _____

2. _____

3. _____

TOP TASK TODAY _____ ☐

WHAT ARE YOU GRATEFUL FOR

Wednesday

1. _____

2. _____

3. _____

TOP TASK TODAY _____ ☐

WHAT ARE YOU GRATEFUL FOR

Thursday

1. _____

2. _____

3. _____

TOP TASK TODAY _____ ☐

"Gratitude is a powerful catalyst for happiness. It's the spark that lights a
fire of joy in your soul." Amy Collette

WHAT ARE YOU GRATEFUL FOR

Friday

1. _____

2. _____

3. _____

TOP TASK TODAY _____ ☐

WHAT ARE YOU GRATEFUL FOR

Saturday

1. _____

2. _____

3. _____

TOP TASK TODAY _____ ☐

WHAT ARE YOU GRATEFUL FOR

Sunday

1. _____

2. _____

3. _____

TOP TASK TODAY _____ ☐

Notes

Week 31

WHAT ARE YOU GRATEFUL FOR

Monday

1. _____

2. _____

3. _____

TOP TASK TODAY _____ ☐

WHAT ARE YOU GRATEFUL FOR

Tuesday

1. _____

2. _____

3. _____

TOP TASK TODAY _____ ☐

WHAT ARE YOU GRATEFUL FOR

Wednesday

1. _____

2. _____

3. _____

TOP TASK TODAY _____ ☐

WHAT ARE YOU GRATEFUL FOR

Thursday

1. _____

2. _____

3. _____

TOP TASK TODAY _____ ☐

"It's up to us to choose contentment and thankfulness now—and to stop imagining that we have to have everything perfect before we'll be happy." Joanna Gaines

/ / 20

Friday

WHAT ARE YOU GRATEFUL FOR

1. _____

2. _____

3. _____

TOP TASK TODAY _____ ☐

Saturday

WHAT ARE YOU GRATEFUL FOR

1. _____

2. _____

3. _____

TOP TASK TODAY _____ ☐

Sunday

WHAT ARE YOU GRATEFUL FOR

1. _____

2. _____

3. _____

TOP TASK TODAY _____ ☐

Notes

Week 32

WHAT ARE YOU GRATEFUL FOR   *Monday*

1. _____

2. _____

3. _____

TOP TASK TODAY _____ ☐

WHAT ARE YOU GRATEFUL FOR   *Tuesday*

1. _____

2. _____

3. _____

TOP TASK TODAY _____ ☐

WHAT ARE YOU GRATEFUL FOR   *Wednesday*

1. _____

2. _____

3. _____

TOP TASK TODAY _____ ☐

WHAT ARE YOU GRATEFUL FOR   *Thursday*

1. _____

2. _____

3. _____

TOP TASK TODAY _____ ☐

"The earlier you learn that you should focus on what you have, and not obsess about what you don't have, the happier you will be." Amy Poehler

WHAT ARE YOU GRATEFUL FOR

Friday

1. _____

2. _____

3. _____

TOP TASK TODAY _____ ☐

WHAT ARE YOU GRATEFUL FOR

Saturday

1. _____

2. _____

3. _____

TOP TASK TODAY _____ ☐

WHAT ARE YOU GRATEFUL FOR

Sunday

1. _____

2. _____

3. _____

TOP TASK TODAY _____ ☐

Notes

Week 33

WHAT ARE YOU GRATEFUL FOR   *Monday*

1. _____

2. _____

3. _____

TOP TASK TODAY _____ ☐

WHAT ARE YOU GRATEFUL FOR   *Tuesday*

1. _____

2. _____

3. _____

TOP TASK TODAY _____ ☐

WHAT ARE YOU GRATEFUL FOR   *Wednesday*

1. _____

2. _____

3. _____

TOP TASK TODAY _____ ☐

WHAT ARE YOU GRATEFUL FOR   *Thursday*

1. _____

2. _____

3. _____

TOP TASK TODAY _____ ☐

"Gratitude is looking on the brighter side of life, even if it means hurting your eyes."
Ellen DeGeneres

WHAT ARE YOU GRATEFUL FOR

Friday

1. _____

2. _____

3. _____

TOP TASK TODAY _____ ☐

WHAT ARE YOU GRATEFUL FOR

Saturday

1. _____

2. _____

3. _____

TOP TASK TODAY _____ ☐

WHAT ARE YOU GRATEFUL FOR

Sunday

1. _____

2. _____

3. _____

TOP TASK TODAY _____ ☐

Notes

Week 34

WHAT ARE YOU GRATEFUL FOR

Monday

1. _____

2. _____

3. _____

TOP TASK TODAY _____ ☐

WHAT ARE YOU GRATEFUL FOR

Tuesday

1. _____

2. _____

3. _____

TOP TASK TODAY _____ ☐

WHAT ARE YOU GRATEFUL FOR

Wednesday

1. _____

2. _____

3. _____

TOP TASK TODAY _____ ☐

WHAT ARE YOU GRATEFUL FOR

Thursday

1. _____

2. _____

3. _____

TOP TASK TODAY _____ ☐

"Appreciation can make a day – even change a life. Your willingness to put in into words is all that is necessary." Margaret Cousins

/ / 20

Friday

WHAT ARE YOU GRATEFUL FOR

1. _____
2. _____
3. _____

TOP TASK TODAY _____ ☐

WHAT ARE YOU GRATEFUL FOR

Saturday

1. _____
2. _____
3. _____

TOP TASK TODAY _____ ☐

WHAT ARE YOU GRATEFUL FOR

Sunday

1. _____
2. _____
3. _____

TOP TASK TODAY _____ ☐

Notes

Week 35

WHAT ARE YOU GRATEFUL FOR

Monday

1. _____

2. _____

3. _____

TOP TASK TODAY _____ ☐

WHAT ARE YOU GRATEFUL FOR

Tuesday

1. _____

2. _____

3. _____

TOP TASK TODAY _____ ☐

WHAT ARE YOU GRATEFUL FOR

Wednesday

1. _____

2. _____

3. _____

TOP TASK TODAY _____ ☐

WHAT ARE YOU GRATEFUL FOR

Thursday

1. _____

2. _____

3. _____

TOP TASK TODAY _____ ☐

"Thank you" is the best prayer that anyone could say. I say that one a lot. Thank you expresses extreme gratitude, humility, understanding." Alice Walker

WHAT ARE YOU GRATEFUL FOR

Friday

1. _____

2. _____

3. _____

TOP TASK TODAY _____ ☐

WHAT ARE YOU GRATEFUL FOR

Saturday

1. _____

2. _____

3. _____

TOP TASK TODAY _____ ☐

WHAT ARE YOU GRATEFUL FOR

Sunday

1. _____

2. _____

3. _____

TOP TASK TODAY _____ ☐

Notes

Week 36

WHAT ARE YOU GRATEFUL FOR

Monday

1. _____

2. _____

3. _____

TOP TASK TODAY _____ ☐

WHAT ARE YOU GRATEFUL FOR

Tuesday

1. _____

2. _____

3. _____

TOP TASK TODAY _____ ☐

WHAT ARE YOU GRATEFUL FOR

Wednesday

1. _____

2. _____

3. _____

TOP TASK TODAY _____ ☐

WHAT ARE YOU GRATEFUL FOR

Thursday

1. _____

2. _____

3. _____

TOP TASK TODAY _____ ☐

"True happiness is not money in the bank or a fancy home-it's a forgiving heart filled with love and gratitude." Charmaine J Forde

WHAT ARE YOU GRATEFUL FOR

Friday

1. _____

2. _____

3. _____

TOP TASK TODAY _____ ☐

WHAT ARE YOU GRATEFUL FOR

Saturday

1. _____

2. _____

3. _____

TOP TASK TODAY _____ ☐

WHAT ARE YOU GRATEFUL FOR

Sunday

1. _____

2. _____

3. _____

TOP TASK TODAY _____ ☐

Notes

Week 37

WHAT ARE YOU GRATEFUL FOR *Monday*

1. _____

2. _____

3. _____

TOP TASK TODAY _____ ☐

WHAT ARE YOU GRATEFUL FOR *Tuesday*

1. _____

2. _____

3. _____

TOP TASK TODAY _____ ☐

WHAT ARE YOU GRATEFUL FOR *Wednesday*

1. _____

2. _____

3. _____

TOP TASK TODAY _____ ☐

WHAT ARE YOU GRATEFUL FOR *Thursday*

1. _____

2. _____

3. _____

TOP TASK TODAY _____ ☐

"Enjoy the little things, for one day you may look back and realize they were the big things." Robert Brault

WHAT ARE YOU GRATEFUL FOR

Friday

1. _____

2. _____

3. _____

TOP TASK TODAY _____ ☐

WHAT ARE YOU GRATEFUL FOR

Saturday

1. _____

2. _____

3. _____

TOP TASK TODAY _____ ☐

WHAT ARE YOU GRATEFUL FOR

Sunday

1. _____

2. _____

3. _____

TOP TASK TODAY _____ ☐

Notes

Week 38

WHAT ARE YOU GRATEFUL FOR   *Monday*

1. _____

2. _____

3. _____

TOP TASK TODAY _____ ☐

WHAT ARE YOU GRATEFUL FOR   *Tuesday*

1. _____

2. _____

3. _____

TOP TASK TODAY _____ ☐

WHAT ARE YOU GRATEFUL FOR   *Wednesday*

1. _____

2. _____

3. _____

TOP TASK TODAY _____ ☐

WHAT ARE YOU GRATEFUL FOR   *Thursday*

1. _____

2. _____

3. _____

TOP TASK TODAY _____ ☐

"If a fellow isn't thankful for what he's got, he isn't likely to be thankful for what he's going to get." Frank A. Clark

WHAT ARE YOU GRATEFUL FOR

Friday

1. _____

2. _____

3. _____

TOP TASK TODAY _____ ☐

WHAT ARE YOU GRATEFUL FOR

Saturday

1. _____

2. _____

3. _____

TOP TASK TODAY _____ ☐

WHAT ARE YOU GRATEFUL FOR

Sunday

1. _____

2. _____

3. _____

TOP TASK TODAY _____ ☐

Notes

Week 39

WHAT ARE YOU GRATEFUL FOR

Monday

1. _____

2. _____

3. _____

TOP TASK TODAY _____ ☐

WHAT ARE YOU GRATEFUL FOR

Tuesday

1. _____

2. _____

3. _____

TOP TASK TODAY _____ ☐

WHAT ARE YOU GRATEFUL FOR

Wednesday

1. _____

2. _____

3. _____

TOP TASK TODAY _____ ☐

WHAT ARE YOU GRATEFUL FOR

Thursday

1. _____

2. _____

3. _____

TOP TASK TODAY _____ ☐

"Gratitude is a currency that we can mint for ourselves, and spend without fear of bankruptcy." Fred De Witt Van Amburgh

Friday

WHAT ARE YOU GRATEFUL FOR

1. _____
2. _____
3. _____

TOP TASK TODAY _____ ☐

Saturday

WHAT ARE YOU GRATEFUL FOR

1. _____
2. _____
3. _____

TOP TASK TODAY _____ ☐

Sunday

WHAT ARE YOU GRATEFUL FOR

1. _____
2. _____
3. _____

TOP TASK TODAY _____ ☐

Notes

Reflections

WHAT HAS YOUR GRATITUDE PRACTICE BROUGHT YOU?

WHAT ARE YOU GOING TO CHANGE?

WHAT'S YOUR NUMBER ONE LESSON?

WHAT WOULD YOU LIKE TO ACHIEVE NEXT?

Week 40

WHAT ARE YOU GRATEFUL FOR   *Monday*

1. _____

2. _____

3. _____

TOP TASK TODAY _____ ☐

WHAT ARE YOU GRATEFUL FOR   *Tuesday*

1. _____

2. _____

3. _____

TOP TASK TODAY _____ ☐

WHAT ARE YOU GRATEFUL FOR   *Wednesday*

1. _____

2. _____

3. _____

TOP TASK TODAY _____ ☐

WHAT ARE YOU GRATEFUL FOR   *Thursday*

1. _____

2. _____

3. _____

TOP TASK TODAY _____ ☐

"The deepest craving of human nature is the need to be appreciated." William James

Friday

WHAT ARE YOU GRATEFUL FOR

1. _____

2. _____

3. _____

TOP TASK TODAY _____ ☐

Saturday

WHAT ARE YOU GRATEFUL FOR

1. _____

2. _____

3. _____

TOP TASK TODAY _____ ☐

Sunday

WHAT ARE YOU GRATEFUL FOR

1. _____

2. _____

3. _____

TOP TASK TODAY _____ ☐

Notes

Week 41

WHAT ARE YOU GRATEFUL FOR

Monday

1. _____

2. _____

3. _____

TOP TASK TODAY _____ ☐

WHAT ARE YOU GRATEFUL FOR

Tuesday

1. _____

2. _____

3. _____

TOP TASK TODAY _____ ☐

WHAT ARE YOU GRATEFUL FOR

Wednesday

1. _____

2. _____

3. _____

TOP TASK TODAY _____ ☐

WHAT ARE YOU GRATEFUL FOR

Thursday

1. _____

2. _____

3. _____

TOP TASK TODAY _____ ☐

"Be thankful for what you have; you'll end up having more. If you concentrate on what you don't have, you will never, ever have enough." Oprah Winfrey

WHAT ARE YOU GRATEFUL FOR

Friday

1. _____

2. _____

3. _____

TOP TASK TODAY _____ ☐

WHAT ARE YOU GRATEFUL FOR

Saturday

1. _____

2. _____

3. _____

TOP TASK TODAY _____ ☐

WHAT ARE YOU GRATEFUL FOR

Sunday

1. _____

2. _____

3. _____

TOP TASK TODAY _____ ☐

Notes

Week 42

WHAT ARE YOU GRATEFUL FOR

Monday

1. _____

2. _____

3. _____

TOP TASK TODAY _____ ☐

WHAT ARE YOU GRATEFUL FOR

Tuesday

1. _____

2. _____

3. _____

TOP TASK TODAY _____ ☐

WHAT ARE YOU GRATEFUL FOR

Wednesday

1. _____

2. _____

3. _____

TOP TASK TODAY _____ ☐

WHAT ARE YOU GRATEFUL FOR

Thursday

1. _____

2. _____

3. _____

TOP TASK TODAY _____ ☐

"Reflect upon your present blessings, of which every man has plenty; not on your past misfortunes, of which all men have some." Charles Dickens

WHAT ARE YOU GRATEFUL FOR

Friday

1. _____

2. _____

3. _____

TOP TASK TODAY _____ ☐

WHAT ARE YOU GRATEFUL FOR

Saturday

1. _____

2. _____

3. _____

TOP TASK TODAY _____ ☐

WHAT ARE YOU GRATEFUL FOR

Sunday

1. _____

2. _____

3. _____

TOP TASK TODAY _____ ☐

Notes

Week 43

WHAT ARE YOU GRATEFUL FOR

Monday

1. _____

2. _____

3. _____

TOP TASK TODAY _____ ☐

WHAT ARE YOU GRATEFUL FOR

Tuesday

1. _____

2. _____

3. _____

TOP TASK TODAY _____ ☐

WHAT ARE YOU GRATEFUL FOR

Wednesday

1. _____

2. _____

3. _____

TOP TASK TODAY _____ ☐

WHAT ARE YOU GRATEFUL FOR

Thursday

1. _____

2. _____

3. _____

TOP TASK TODAY _____ ☐

"You cannot do a kindness too soon because you never know how soon it will be too late."
Ralph Waldo Emerson

WHAT ARE YOU GRATEFUL FOR

Friday

1. _____

2. _____

3. _____

TOP TASK TODAY _____ ☐

WHAT ARE YOU GRATEFUL FOR

Saturday

1. _____

2. _____

3. _____

TOP TASK TODAY _____ ☐

WHAT ARE YOU GRATEFUL FOR

Sunday

1. _____

2. _____

3. _____

TOP TASK TODAY _____ ☐

Notes

Week 44

WHAT ARE YOU GRATEFUL FOR

Monday

1. _____

2. _____

3. _____

TOP TASK TODAY _____ ☐

WHAT ARE YOU GRATEFUL FOR

Tuesday

1. _____

2. _____

3. _____

TOP TASK TODAY _____ ☐

WHAT ARE YOU GRATEFUL FOR

Wednesday

1. _____

2. _____

3. _____

TOP TASK TODAY _____ ☐

WHAT ARE YOU GRATEFUL FOR

Thursday

1. _____

2. _____

3. _____

TOP TASK TODAY _____ ☐

"Ralph Waldo Emerson When I started counting my blessings,
my whole life turned around." Willie Nelson

WHAT ARE YOU GRATEFUL FOR

Friday

1. _____

2. _____

3. _____

TOP TASK TODAY _____ ☐

WHAT ARE YOU GRATEFUL FOR

Saturday

1. _____

2. _____

3. _____

TOP TASK TODAY _____ ☐

WHAT ARE YOU GRATEFUL FOR

Sunday

1. _____

2. _____

3. _____

TOP TASK TODAY _____ ☐

Notes

Week 45

WHAT ARE YOU GRATEFUL FOR

Monday

1. _____

2. _____

3. _____

TOP TASK TODAY _____ ☐

WHAT ARE YOU GRATEFUL FOR

Tuesday

1. _____

2. _____

3. _____

TOP TASK TODAY _____ ☐

WHAT ARE YOU GRATEFUL FOR

Wednesday

1. _____

2. _____

3. _____

TOP TASK TODAY _____ ☐

WHAT ARE YOU GRATEFUL FOR

Thursday

1. _____

2. _____

3. _____

TOP TASK TODAY _____ ☐

"Gratitude and attitude are not challenges; they are choices."
Robert Braathe

WHAT ARE YOU GRATEFUL FOR

Friday

1. _____

2. _____

3. _____

TOP TASK TODAY _____ ☐

WHAT ARE YOU GRATEFUL FOR

Saturday

1. _____

2. _____

3. _____

TOP TASK TODAY _____ ☐

WHAT ARE YOU GRATEFUL FOR

Sunday

1. _____

2. _____

3. _____

TOP TASK TODAY _____ ☐

Notes

Week 46

WHAT ARE YOU GRATEFUL FOR

Monday

1. _____

2. _____

3. _____

TOP TASK TODAY _____ ☐

WHAT ARE YOU GRATEFUL FOR

Tuesday

1. _____

2. _____

3. _____

TOP TASK TODAY _____ ☐

WHAT ARE YOU GRATEFUL FOR

Wednesday

1. _____

2. _____

3. _____

TOP TASK TODAY _____ ☐

WHAT ARE YOU GRATEFUL FOR

Thursday

1. _____

2. _____

3. _____

TOP TASK TODAY _____ ☐

"In life, one has a choice to take one of two paths: to wait for some special day-or to celebrate each special day." Rasheed Ogunlaru

WHAT ARE YOU GRATEFUL FOR

Friday

1. _____

2. _____

3. _____

TOP TASK TODAY _____ ☐

WHAT ARE YOU GRATEFUL FOR

Saturday

1. _____

2. _____

3. _____

TOP TASK TODAY _____ ☐

WHAT ARE YOU GRATEFUL FOR

Sunday

1. _____

2. _____

3. _____

TOP TASK TODAY _____ ☐

Notes

Week 47

WHAT ARE YOU GRATEFUL FOR
Monday

1. _____

2. _____

3. _____

TOP TASK TODAY _____ ☐

WHAT ARE YOU GRATEFUL FOR
Tuesday

1. _____

2. _____

3. _____

TOP TASK TODAY _____ ☐

WHAT ARE YOU GRATEFUL FOR
Wednesday

1. _____

2. _____

3. _____

TOP TASK TODAY _____ ☐

WHAT ARE YOU GRATEFUL FOR
Thursday

1. _____

2. _____

3. _____

TOP TASK TODAY _____ ☐

"Peace is the result of retraining your mind to process life as it is, rather than as you think it should be." Dr. Wayne Dyer

WHAT ARE YOU GRATEFUL FOR

Friday

1. _____

2. _____

3. _____

TOP TASK TODAY _____ ☐

WHAT ARE YOU GRATEFUL FOR

Saturday

1. _____

2. _____

3. _____

TOP TASK TODAY _____ ☐

WHAT ARE YOU GRATEFUL FOR

Sunday

1. _____

2. _____

3. _____

TOP TASK TODAY _____ ☐

Notes

Week 48

WHAT ARE YOU GRATEFUL FOR

Monday

1. _____

2. _____

3. _____

TOP TASK TODAY _____ ☐

WHAT ARE YOU GRATEFUL FOR

Tuesday

1. _____

2. _____

3. _____

TOP TASK TODAY _____ ☐

WHAT ARE YOU GRATEFUL FOR

Wednesday

1. _____

2. _____

3. _____

TOP TASK TODAY _____ ☐

WHAT ARE YOU GRATEFUL FOR

Thursday

1. _____

2. _____

3. _____

TOP TASK TODAY _____ ☐

"Things turn out best for people who make the best of the way things turn out."
John Wooden

WHAT ARE YOU GRATEFUL FOR

Friday

1. _____

2. _____

3. _____

TOP TASK TODAY _____ ☐

WHAT ARE YOU GRATEFUL FOR

Saturday

1. _____

2. _____

3. _____

TOP TASK TODAY _____ ☐

WHAT ARE YOU GRATEFUL FOR

Sunday

1. _____

2. _____

3. _____

TOP TASK TODAY _____ ☐

Notes

Week 49

WHAT ARE YOU GRATEFUL FOR   *Monday*

1. _____

2. _____

3. _____

TOP TASK TODAY _____ ☐

WHAT ARE YOU GRATEFUL FOR   *Tuesday*

1. _____

2. _____

3. _____

TOP TASK TODAY _____ ☐

WHAT ARE YOU GRATEFUL FOR   *Wednesday*

1. _____

2. _____

3. _____

TOP TASK TODAY _____ ☐

WHAT ARE YOU GRATEFUL FOR   *Thursday*

1. _____

2. _____

3. _____

TOP TASK TODAY _____ ☐

"Things turn out best for people who make the best of the way things turn out."
John Wooden

WHAT ARE YOU GRATEFUL FOR

Friday

1. _____

2. _____

3. _____

TOP TASK TODAY _____ ☐

WHAT ARE YOU GRATEFUL FOR

Saturday

1. _____

2. _____

3. _____

TOP TASK TODAY _____ ☐

WHAT ARE YOU GRATEFUL FOR

Sunday

1. _____

2. _____

3. _____

TOP TASK TODAY _____ ☐

Notes

Week 50

WHAT ARE YOU GRATEFUL FOR

Monday

1. _____

2. _____

3. _____

TOP TASK TODAY _____ ☐

WHAT ARE YOU GRATEFUL FOR

Tuesday

1. _____

2. _____

3. _____

TOP TASK TODAY _____ ☐

WHAT ARE YOU GRATEFUL FOR

Wednesday

1. _____

2. _____

3. _____

TOP TASK TODAY _____ ☐

WHAT ARE YOU GRATEFUL FOR

Thursday

1. _____

2. _____

3. _____

TOP TASK TODAY _____ ☐

"It is impossible to feel grateful and depressed in the same moment." Naomi Williams

WHAT ARE YOU GRATEFUL FOR

Friday

1. _____

2. _____

3. _____

TOP TASK TODAY _____ ☐

WHAT ARE YOU GRATEFUL FOR

Saturday

1. _____

2. _____

3. _____

TOP TASK TODAY _____ ☐

WHAT ARE YOU GRATEFUL FOR

Sunday

1. _____

2. _____

3. _____

TOP TASK TODAY _____ ☐

Notes

Week 51

WHAT ARE YOU GRATEFUL FOR

Monday

1. _____

2. _____

3. _____

TOP TASK TODAY _____ ☐

WHAT ARE YOU GRATEFUL FOR

Tuesday

1. _____

2. _____

3. _____

TOP TASK TODAY _____ ☐

WHAT ARE YOU GRATEFUL FOR

Wednesday

1. _____

2. _____

3. _____

TOP TASK TODAY _____ ☐

WHAT ARE YOU GRATEFUL FOR

Thursday

1. _____

2. _____

3. _____

TOP TASK TODAY _____ ☐

"When you are grateful, fear disappears and abundance appears."
Anthony Robbins

Friday

WHAT ARE YOU GRATEFUL FOR

1. _____

2. _____

3. _____

TOP TASK TODAY _____ ☐

Saturday

WHAT ARE YOU GRATEFUL FOR

1. _____

2. _____

3. _____

TOP TASK TODAY _____ ☐

Sunday

WHAT ARE YOU GRATEFUL FOR

1. _____

2. _____

3. _____

TOP TASK TODAY _____ ☐

Notes

Week 52

WHAT ARE YOU GRATEFUL FOR

Monday

1. _____

2. _____

3. _____

TOP TASK TODAY _____ ☐

WHAT ARE YOU GRATEFUL FOR

Tuesday

1. _____

2. _____

3. _____

TOP TASK TODAY _____ ☐

WHAT ARE YOU GRATEFUL FOR

Wednesday

1. _____

2. _____

3. _____

TOP TASK TODAY _____ ☐

WHAT ARE YOU GRATEFUL FOR

Thursday

1. _____

2. _____

3. _____

TOP TASK TODAY _____ ☐

"What's meant for you won't pass you."
Christine Kellegher, my Nan.

/ / 20

Friday

WHAT ARE YOU GRATEFUL FOR

1. _____

2. _____

3. _____

TOP TASK TODAY _____ ☐

Saturday

WHAT ARE YOU GRATEFUL FOR

1. _____

2. _____

3. _____

TOP TASK TODAY _____ ☐

Sunday

WHAT ARE YOU GRATEFUL FOR

1. _____

2. _____

3. _____

TOP TASK TODAY _____ ☐

Notes

Reflections

HOW HAS GRATITUDE POSITIVELY CHANGED YOUR LIFE?

WOULD YOU RECOMMEND PRACTICING GRATITUDE TO A FRIEND?

I would love to hear your feedback on your journey with
'My Gratitude Attitude Journal' and anything you feel I can do better.

I would be very grateful if you send your ideas for improvement to
karen@mygratitudeattitudejournal.com

Thank you for taking the time to be grateful,

Karen
Dwyer
XX